KU-099-409

HEINEMANN Profiles

Mother Teresa

Haydn Middleton

First published in Great Britain by Heinemann
Library, Halley Court, Jordan Hill, Oxford
OX2 8EJ, a division of Reed Educational and
Professional Publishing Ltd.
Heinemann is a registered trademark of Reed
Educational & Professional Publishing Limited.

OXFORD MELBOURNE AUCKLAND
JOHANNESBURG BLANTYRE
GABORONE IBADAN PORTSMOUTH
NH (USA) CHICAGO

Designed by Visual Image
Originated by Dot Gradations
Printed and bound in Hong Kong/China

04 03 02 01 00
10 9 8 7 6 5 4 3 2 1

ISBN 0 431 08632 X

**British Library Cataloguing
in Publication Data**

Middleton, Haydn
Mother Teresa. – (Heinemann Profiles)
1. Teresa, Mother, 1910–1997 – Juvenile
   literature 2. Women missionaries – India
   – Biography – Juvenile literature 3.
   Missionaries – India – Biography –
   Juvenile literature
I. Title
266.2'092
ISBN 043108632X

Acknowledgements
The Publishers would like to thank the following
for permission to reproduce photographs: AKG
Photo: p6; Associated Press: pp4, 5, 12, 20, 35, 45,
47, 51, 53; BBC: p32; Corbis: Hulton-Deutsch
p22; Rex Features: pp25, 28, 33, 36, 40, 42, Jobard
p49, D Ludwig p46, J Rogers p43; Sipa Press: R
Trippett p37; Trip: J Randall p14, H Rogers
pp26, 31, B Turner p39.

Cover photograph reproduced with permission of
Rex Features

Every effort has been made to contact copyright
holders of any material reproduced in this book.
Any omissions will be rectified in subsequent
printings if notice is given to the Publisher.

For more information about Heinemann Library
books, or to order, please phone ++44 (0)1865
888066, or send a fax to ++44 (0)1865 314091.
You can visit our website at
www.heinemann.co.uk.

Any words appearing in the text in bold, **like
this**, are explained in the Glossary.

CONTENTS

WHO WAS MOTHER TERESA?

Mother Teresa of Calcutta (1910–97), the 'Saint of the Slums', never claimed to be anyone special. When people wanted to write her **biography**, she could not understand why. 'I am just a little pencil in God's hand,' she would say. She devoted most of her life to helping 'the poorest of the poor', first in India and afterwards in many other countries. Until the 1960s she was not well known outside India. Then the **media** made her world famous and she won a great number of prizes and awards for her work. In 1979 she was awarded the **prestigious** Nobel Peace Prize, which she received with her usual humility.

Mother Teresa
in old age.

SAINT OR SINNER?

For years Mother Teresa was seen as a living, breathing saint. British journalist Christopher Hitchens once called her 'the least criticized human being on Earth'. That all changed towards the end of her life. In the late twentieth century, the world was a very different place from the one in which Mother Teresa had begun her work. In the 1990s some people accused her of not

An opponent of abortion, Mother Teresa believed that 'there can never be enough' children.

keeping up with the times. On issues such as abortion, technology, women's rights and poverty relief they called her views old-fashioned and even cruel. At her death in 1997 she was saluted as one of the world's great **humanitarians** but the debate continues about the true impact and value of her work.

'Mother Teresa inspired many people with whom she came into contact not because she preached powerful sermons but because she demonstrated a way, not always effective, of using the power of love as a force for healing and **redemption**. In spite of all the criticism levelled against her, Mother Teresa gave tens of thousands of people the opportunity to express their love for their fellow human beings.'   From *Mother Teresa: Beyond the Image* by Anne Sebba, 1997

BALKAN BEGINNINGS

Mother Teresa won fame for her work in Calcutta, a huge city in India. She became an Indian citizen in 1949 but she was not an Indian by birth, nor was her real name Teresa. That was the name she took on becoming a nun. She was born on 26 August 1910, in a war-torn south-eastern part of Europe known as the **Balkans**. Her Roman Catholic parents, Nikola and Drana Bojaxhiu, already had two children: Age, a girl and Lazar, a boy. On the day after the new baby was born, she was christened Agnes Gonxha.

The market place at Skopje early in the twentieth century.

Skopje

Around the time that Agnes was born, a traveller described the town of Skopje this way: 'Tombstones are always the prominent feature of a Turkish town but Skopje resembles an oasis in a desert of the dead. Acres of them in general disorder, a few erect but mostly toppling or fallen, surround the town and stretch long arms into it: they flank the main road and dot the side streets and far out into the country… The sight is gruesome and one's mind pictures the many massacres that have made this sea of silent slabs.'

'Mine was a happy family,' Mother Teresa said in later life. 'I had one brother and one sister, but I do not like to talk about it. It is not important now. The important thing is to follow God's way, the way he leads us to do something beautiful for him.' It is not easy to discover details about the early life of Agnes Gonxha. Her home town of Skopje is now in a country called Macedonia. When Agnes was born it was a part of the Turkish Empire.

LIVING CLOSE TO DEATH

The Bojaxhiu family was neither Macedonian nor Turkish, but Albanian. For hundreds of years the Albanian people had no country of their own and many of them, like Agnes' father, campaigned for an **independent** homeland. In 1912, after a war in the Balkans, a small Albania was created but half the Albanian population – including the Bojaxhius – could not be fitted into it.

GONXHA THE GIRL

Gonxha means 'flower bud', and that was what Agnes' family usually called her. Albanians today still know her by this name. Although she was not brilliant at school work, she was a keen singer and a good mandolin player. Her older brother Lazar said she was sensible, serious and deeply religious even as a little girl. She would tell him off whenever he helped himself to jam during the night, because they were not supposed to touch food after midnight if they were going to attend **mass** and **communion** with their mother in the morning.

CHANGING FAMILY FORTUNES

Agnes (arrowed) with her Skopje school friends at the age of ten.

Her father Nikola was a successful businessman and his work often took him abroad. Agnes liked to hear his stories about his travels. Maybe it gave her an appetite to see the world for herself when she was

older. Nikola also continued to campaign for a Greater Albania in which all the Albanian people could live together. This made him enemies in the **Balkans**; after a political dinner in 1918 he suddenly died – possibly from poisoning.

Times were hard for the Bojaxhiu family after Nikola's death. Agnes' mother Drana made ends meet by setting up her own embroidery and textile business. But although she was poor herself, she still helped those who were poorer. As a child, Agnes thought the regular guests at mealtimes were relatives. Later she discovered that they were complete strangers. Her **devout** mother's kindness and **hospitality** made a great impression on the growing girl. So did this piece of advice which she gave to her children: 'When you do good, do it quietly, as if you were throwing a stone into the sea.'

'I remember my mother, my father and the rest of us praying together each evening… It is God's greatest gift to the family. It maintains family unity. The family that does not pray together does not stay together.'
Mother Teresa

Agnes (seated) with Age and Lazar in 1924.

IN AND OUT OF CHURCH

The Roman Catholic church of the Sacred Heart in Skopje played an important part in the life of the Bojaxhiu family. They worshipped there, and both Agnes and her sister Age sang sweetly in the church choir, even though Agnes had a weak chest and often suffered with chronic coughs. According to Lazar, his mother and sisters seemed to live as much in the church as they did at home.

Every year, groups of local Catholics and non–Catholics would make a **pilgrimage** to the chapel of the Madonna of Letnice. Agnes' mother arranged for her to visit the shrine at other times, too – to pray alone in the chapel.

Agnes, right of her sister, Age (with parasol), on a visit to Nerezima.

Joy…is a compass

Unlike many women who become nuns, Agnes had no sudden vision to convince her of what she had to do. When she asked Father Jambrekovic if God really was calling her, he answered that if she felt joy, then that might mean it was a true call. 'Joy that comes from the depths of your being,' he told her, 'is like a compass by which you can tell what direction your life should follow.'

HOW COULD SHE BE SURE?

Even at the age of twelve, Agnes took comfort and strength from prayer. Already she sensed that perhaps she would become a nun in later life and devote her life to God – perhaps through teaching – but she needed to be sure about taking such a big step.

As she grew older, she had many talks about her future with two important members of the Church. One was Monsignor Janez Gnidovec. He was Bishop of Skopje from 1924 to 1939 and a close friend of the Bojaxhiu family. The other was Father Franjo Jambrekovic, who became **pastor** of the Sacred Heart in 1925. As well as starting a library, he set up a Christian youth group called the **Sodality** of the Blessed Virgin Mary, which greatly inspired Agnes. He also stirred the girl's interest in the work of **missionaries** in India.

In October 1981 an Australian journalist asked whether the 'mother of thousands' missed having a child of her own. 'Naturally, naturally, of course,' she replied. 'That is the sacrifice we make. That is the gift we give to God.'

'WHAT WILL I DO FOR CHRIST?'

Father Jambrekovic told the girls of the **Sodality** about the **Jesuits**. The Jesuit Order was founded in 1534 by Ignatius Loyola, a Spanish Catholic, who later became a saint. Its original aims were to protect Catholicism against the **Protestant Reformation** and to carry out **missionary** work. Agnes learned from Father Jambrekovic that Jesuit missionaries had left the **Balkans** for Bengal, India, in 1924. That stirred her imagination. She also thought hard about these questions in Loyola's book, *Spiritual Exercises*: 'What have I done for Christ, what am I doing for Christ and what will I do for Christ?'. She began to feel quite sure that Christ was calling her to serve him as a missionary nun.

THE NEED FOR SELF-SACRIFICE

Deciding to be a nun is not really like choosing to be an artist or an athlete. Agnes believed that if she truly was being called, then she had no choice in the matter at all. God's will simply had to be done. And that meant accepting that she would never marry or have her own family – since nuns regard Christ as their husband. This was not easy, because Agnes had always liked children. Nonetheless, she finally told her mother that she would become a nun. Drana could hardly have been surprised by her daughter's decision. 'Put your hand in His,' she told Agnes, 'and walk all the way with Him.'

Agnes also wrote with her news to her brother Lazar, an army officer who was about to become an **equerry** to the new King Zog of Albania. He wrote back, asking a little sharply if she really knew what she was doing. 'You think you are important because you are an officer serving a king with two million subjects,' Agnes replied. 'But I am serving the King of the whole world.'

IRISH INTERLUDE

Agnes chose to join the Loreto Sisters – the branch in Rathfarnham, Ireland of one of the leading **orders** of nuns: the Institute of the Blessed Virgin Mary (IBVM).

Teresa of Lisieux

There are two notable Saint Teresas in the Roman Catholic Church. The more famous is Teresa of Avila (1515–82), an **aristocratic** Spanish nun whose spiritual writings are still read by many today. But Agnes named herself after the lesser-known Teresa of Lisieux (1873–97), the daughter of a French watchmaker. This good-natured 'Little Flower', who died at the age of 24, inspired others with her deep but simple faith in God. She believed that it was possible to serve God by doing the most ordinary little jobs cheerfully and well.

She knew that nuns from this **order** were often sent as **missionaries** to India. In September 1928, at the age of eighteen, she left home for Zagreb, where she was joined by Betika Kajnc, another young woman who wished to become a Loreto Sister.

They did not go directly to Loreto Abbey at Rathfarnham. First they travelled by train to Paris, where they were interviewed by Mother Eugene MacAvin. She was impressed with their seriousness, so she sent them on, with her recommendation, to Ireland.

A CHANGE OF NAME

At Loreto Abbey, Agnes began training to be a nun. As well as finding out about the work of the order, she started to learn English. This would be useful when she moved on to India, because in 1928 that huge country was still a part of the British Empire, in which English was the official language. Although she had been Agnes Bojaxhiu for so long, she took the religious name of Sister Teresa. In many ways, she was breaking completely with her past.

This photo of Agnes (top) at her school graduation was taken in 1928, when she was 18, shortly before she left to join the Loreto Sisters in Ireland. Her mother and sister were never to see her again.

INTO INDIA

In December 1928, Sister Teresa set off on the voyage that had been in her mind for so many years. It was a long trip: through the Suez Canal, the Red Sea, the Indian Ocean and into the Bay of Bengal. The street scenes – and the poverty – that she found in India were a world away from Skopje.

'A GREAT GIRL FULL OF FUN'

In Darjeeling, at the foot of the Himalayas, Teresa began her novitiate – the first steps a nun must make towards taking her final **vows**. She taught at the Loreto convent school there, and helped out at

Sister Teresa (left) with another **novice** nun at Darjeeling in 1929. The heavy black **habit** must have been uncomfortable to wear in India's hot climate.

First impressions

Sister Teresa's first impressions of India were so strong that she had to write them down. Of the city of Madras, she wrote: 'Many families live in the streets, along the city walls, even in places thronged with people. Day and night they live out in the open on mats they have made from large palm leaves – or frequently on the bare ground. They are all virtually naked, wearing at best a ragged loincloth… As we went along the street we chanced upon one family gathered around a dead relation, wrapped in worn red rags, strewn with yellow flowers, his face painted in coloured stripes. It was a horrifying scene. If our people could only see all this, they would stop grumbling about their own misfortunes and offer thanks to God for blessing them with such abundance.'

the small medical station, where she found almost unbelievable suffering. Another nun, who arrived in India a year before her, later remembered Teresa as a 'great girl, very jolly and bright, full of fun… She didn't know much English in those days but it was marvellous how she picked it up. She was always a great worker too. Very hard-working. She was also a very kind and **charitable** sort of person even as a young nun.' Sometimes she was teased for praying so hard and so often – and also for being so clumsy at lighting the candles for **Benediction**!

Sister Teresa in 1931, soon after she had taken her first vows.

'CITY OF DREADFUL NIGHT'

In 1931 Teresa took her first **vows** of poverty, **chastity** and obedience. During this ceremony, she had to lie for some time with her face to the floor, as if she were dead. It was meant to show that she was leaving behind all worldly desires. Soon afterwards she left Darjeeling behind too, to begin her teaching career in Calcutta – a place which the English writer Rudyard Kipling, creator of *The Jungle Book*, had once called the 'City of Dreadful Night'.

IN AND OUT OF THE CONVENT

Although she lived in a slum area of Calcutta, for many years Teresa saw little of the suffering on the streets around her. High walls separated her convent **compound** from the rest of the city. Teresa taught in English at Loreto Entally, a boarding school for girls from broken homes, orphans and children with only one parent. She also taught geography, then history, in the Bengali language at St Mary's school nearby. She was a lively and well-liked teacher and, soon after she took her final lifetime vows in 1937, she became Principal of St Mary's.

'Dear child, do not forget that you went to India for the sake of the poor.'
a reminder for Teresa in a letter from her mother

There was then a huge upheaval as World War Two (1939–45) raged and India took its often violent path to **independence**. Teresa began to wonder if God was calling her to work for Him beyond the safety of the convent walls.

A festering labyrinth…

The writer Rumer Godden lived in Calcutta from the mid-1920s until 1939. Away from the huge city's smarter areas, she later recalled:

a festering labyrinth of little narrow streets… people living on pavements, whole **Eurasian** families in two rooms with very little furniture, and a naked light bulb. The meat safe was usually on a shady wall to keep all the food in. It was very squalid. The streets were crowded with lepers, begging all amongst the people, **smallpox** was rampant and you did see babies in dustbins. What was horrifying then was that no one did anything about it.

Rumer Godden in conversation with Anne Sebba, 1995

'A Call within a Call'

Teresa heard this 'call within a call', as she described it, on 10 September 1946, when she was 36 years old. (The sisters of the **order** that Teresa later founded now celebrate this date every year as 'Inspiration Day'.) She discussed her new aim with a **Jesuit** priest, Father Celeste Van Exem. He could see how badly she wished to leave the teaching order, to care for the people of the slums and maybe start an order of her own for that purpose. 'She was not an exceptional person,' he recalled. 'She was an ordinary Loreto nun, a very ordinary person, but with a great love for her Lord.'

A period of probation

It was no small matter for a nun to be released from the convent to work on the streets of Calcutta.

Indians celebrate the end of their long struggle for independence from Great Britain. Mother Teresa was just beginning her struggle against poverty.

The message was clear

'This is how it happened,' Teresa told her spiritual director, Father Julien Henry. 'I was travelling to Darjeeling by train, when I heard the voice of God.' Father Henry then asked her how she had heard His voice above the noise of a rattling train and she had replied, with a smile, 'I was sure it was God's voice. I was certain that He was calling me. The message was clear. I must leave the convent to help the poor by living among them. This was a command, something to be done, something definite. I knew where I had to be. But I did not know how to get there.'

From *Mother Teresa – Beyond the Image* by Anne Sebba, 1997

Teresa had to wait until July 1948 to hear that the church **authorities** had granted her wish – but only for one year. She still had to keep her nun's **vows** of poverty, **chastity** and obedience, but now she had twelve months to prove that she could do useful work in the teeming city.

She spent some time learning basic nursing skills with the Medical Mission Sisters in Patna. She found out how to give an injection, deliver a baby and make beds with hospital corners. Here too she changed from her **habit** into a cheap white cotton **sari**, which was far more practical in the heat. This was to become Teresa's uniform for her new life – a life that began when she returned to Calcutta, alone but full of determination to succeed, in December 1948.

Calcutta is the
largest city in
eastern India.
Many of its 11
million people
live in extreme
poverty.

'THE POOREST OF THE POOR'

Now that Teresa was free to work in the **bustees** or slums of Calcutta, what was she to do? At first she did what she knew best – teaching. In the area called Moti Jhil she gathered a group of keen children around her and taught them by writing in the mud with a big stick. Neither then nor later was Teresa the greatest forward-planner in the world. She firmly believed that, as long as she was obeying God's call, He would always direct her.

A NEW HOME

For some time, Teresa slept little. She often wandered the streets at night, giving help to whoever needed it. 'Oh God!' she wrote in her diary, 'If I cannot help these people in their poverty and their suffering, let me at least die with them, close to them so that in that way I can show them your love.' Things improved in February 1949, when she moved into a room in a large house at 14 Creek Lane. Its owner, a Roman Catholic Indian called Michael Gomes, asked for no rent from her, nor money for the food he provided. Teresa's first full-time helper – a widow called Charur Ma – soon joined her there. More and more children came to be taught, so she rented a hut for the lessons.

Many of the older priests thought Teresa was mad to be living among the very poor. Several young women, however, were inspired by her example. They came to help her, sometimes leaving school before their final exams to do so. Teresa showed in that first year that her work could be worthwhile. At the end of 1949, she became an Indian citizen, then applied to the Pope in Rome to set up a new **order** of her own to continue the job she had begun.

'Our object is to quench the thirst of Jesus Christ on the cross by dedicating ourselves freely to serve the poorest of the poor, according to the work and teaching of our Lord… Our special task will be to proclaim Jesus Christ to all peoples, above all to those who are in our care. We call ourselves **Missionaries** of Charity.'

From the constitution of Teresa's new order

MISSIONARIES OF CHARITY

On 7 October 1950 the Pope gave Teresa permission to set up her new **order**. Like other nuns, the **Missionaries** of Charity took **vows** of poverty, **chastity** and obedience, but they also vowed 'to give wholehearted and free service to the poorest of the poor'. According to Teresa, 'to be able to love the poor and know the poor we must be poor ourselves.' So, like her, the sisters were allowed very few possessions. They dressed in simple white cotton **saris** bordered in blue (the colour of the Virgin Mary), with a cross pinned to the left

From the start, the Missionaries of Charity led strictly organized days.

- ○ 4.40   Rise
- ○ 5.00   Prayers followed by **Mass** and sermon, followed by breakfast and cleaning
- ○ 8.00   Work among poor and needy
- ○ 12.30 Lunch followed by short rest
- 2.30   Reading and meditation
- ○ 3.00   Tea
- 3.15   Adoration of the Blessed Sacrament
- ○ 4.30   Afternoon service to the poor followed by supper
- ○ 9.00   Evening prayers
- 9.45   Bed
- ○

'God in distressing disguise'

'We know now,' Mother Teresa once said, 'that being unwanted is the greatest disease of all.' The aim of her order was to make everyone feel wanted: babies thrown away on rubbish heaps, the old left to die alone, the mentally ill, every kind of outcast from society, whatever their race or religion. Teresa said that in each of these people she saw 'God Himself, in distressing disguise.'

shoulder. As head of this new order, Sister Teresa now became Mother Teresa.

Mother Teresa among her Missionaries of Charity.

Her **idealism** appealed strongly to many young Indian women, who were keen to make their world a better place. Soon 14 Creek Lane was too small to contain all the new recruits, and a new headquarters, or 'Mother House', was set up at 54a Lower Circular Road. It was bought very cheaply from a Muslim, with money authorized by the Archbishop. More and more free schools were started too. Slowly but surely, the Missionaries of Charity were making their presence felt. And as more people got to hear about them, the more **donations** they gave to help the order's work.

A view from the
outside of the
building which
houses Nirmal
Hriday.

A HOME FOR THE DYING

Indian Hindus see death in a different way from
Christians. They link it with impurity and pollution,
and only people known as **untouchables** are meant
to handle corpses. Often when the poor were on
the point of death, they could be thrown out of
their lodgings to die – and so save the house from
being 'tainted'. Mother Teresa was dismayed to see
so many people ending their lives on the streets. Her
Sisters tended them as best they could, but she
begged the Calcutta Corporation to find a place
where they could 'die with dignity and love'.

NIRMAL HRIDAY

In August 1952 Mother Teresa got what she wanted:
a 'home for the dying' – which she called Nirmal

Hriday (Place of the Pure Heart) — at the sacred Hindu site of Kalighat. 'There were a lot of **destitutes**,' recalled an Indian Medical Service Officer in 1979, 'and Mother Teresa and her band of helpers would go into the streets and pick them up to die with dignity. She did a lot of good work for people but more important and significantly she set an example to the local Hindu population, who were normally only interested in their own family members.'

Sometimes, however, Mother Teresa disagreed with her medical helpers at Nirmal Hriday. Many of the sick could not be saved, but some were suffering from diseases such as malnutrition, which could actually be treated. Mother Teresa did not always see the difference. A visitor once saw the Sisters ask her to save a boy of sixteen who was on the verge of death, but she simply blessed him and said, 'Never mind, it's a lovely day to go to Heaven.'

A ruthless woman?

Dr Marcus Fernandes worked as a volunteer at Nirmal Hriday. His wife Patricia later worked on several of Mother Teresa's projects. In 1994 she recalled, 'I met Mother Teresa on many occasions… My assessment… was that she was an extremely ruthless and hard woman… My husband had quite severe differences of opinion with her and she would never listen or take any advice on anything… She could only cope with uneducated people, the sort she could shout orders at.'

BRANCHING OUT

In 1955 Mother Teresa started a children's home, called Shishu Bavan, in a rented building just a block away from the Mother House. By 1958 there were facilities for 90 homeless, abandoned, sick or deprived children. At first she accepted a government **grant** to help pay for this, but the government insisted that she spend exactly 33 **rupees** on each child. Soon she stopped taking this money, since she wanted to take in more children and spend only 17 rupees on each one. As a result, some of her critics said she was 'spreading herself

One of the wards in Nirmal Hriday.

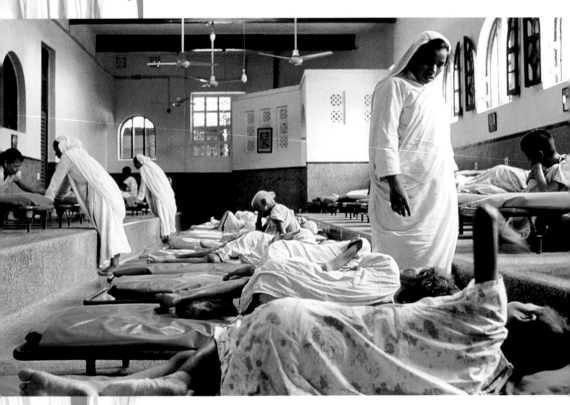

too thinly' – trying to do too much for too many and so not making a *big* difference to those she did help. 'But there are so many needing help,' was her reply. Often the children were tiny babies, left to die by families who could not cope.

TAKING TREATMENT TO THE SUFFERING

Early in 1956, financed by US$5000 from Catholic Relief Services in New York, the **Missionaries** set up their first mobile clinic. This converted van went into some of the city's poorest areas, providing free medical services. Then, in the next year, another mobile clinic was set up – this time for Calcutta's 30,000 lepers. Carrying medicines and equipment, it visited four centres every week in the **bustee** areas of Howrah, Tiljala, Dhappa and Moti Jhil. A year later the number of stations visited had risen to eight. But already by the late 1950s, Mother Teresa was beginning to look beyond Calcutta, even beyond India.

Mother Teresa masterminded the order's expansion with great energy, but she remained as calm as ever despite all the demands made on her.

'What I admired most in Mother Teresa was that she never gave the feeling of being harassed or stressed; that was a big motivation. In the days before she travelled, she always had time for everyone.'
Lady Aruna Paul, 1995

OVERSEAS EXPANSION

According to Roman Catholic law, new **orders** must wait for ten years before opening other houses. Mother Teresa's order was ten years old in 1960 – when she herself was fifty. In that year she had 119 Sisters, mostly Indian, following her **rule** but she was keen to spread her message further. So she sent groups of sisters to begin similar work in the states of Bihar and Uttar Pradesh, and in India's capital city Delhi. In the following years more homes and services were set up all over India. After introducing a mobile clinic leprosy service at Asansol, West Bengal, a town for lepers – Shanti Nagar – was founded.

'POOR ON THE MOON'

By 1960 people overseas were getting to hear about Mother Teresa and her work. Her fame increased after she went abroad to address the National Council for Catholic Women in Las Vegas, USA. From there, she travelled widely in the USA and Europe before returning to India. Although she was not a gifted public speaker – and she never spoke English fluently – she impressed many people by her simple sincerity. Although she never begged for money for her work – saying that she depended upon God to provide – people still contributed very generously.

On her travels, she saw that the poor needed help even in supposedly **affluent** countries. In 1965 Pope Paul VI gave her permission to set up homes in these countries, too. The first, in Corocote, Venezuela, was opened in July 1965. In 1968 one was opened in the slums of Rome and in 1969 a centre for Aborigines was started at Bourke, Australia. Throughout the 1970s, every six months or so a new **Missionaries** of Charity centre would appear somewhere in the world. 'If there are poor on the moon, we shall go there too,' Mother Teresa promised.

Patients in Calcutta queue to see a doctor at a clinic.

'SOMETHING BEAUTIFUL FOR GOD'

By the late 1960s, Mother Teresa was quite well known all over the world, especially among Roman Catholics. Then two BBC TV **documentaries** introduced her to millions more people. The first was *Meeting Point* (1968), when she was interviewed by British journalist Malcolm Muggeridge in London. Small and wrinkled, the old nun spoke simply but movingly about her work. She made no appeal for money but between £9000 and £25,000 was sent in by viewers.

WITNESSING A MIRACLE?

The second TV programme, again made by Muggeridge and a BBC crew but this time in Calcutta, had an even greater impact. At first Mother

In the 1960s many western people began to look to India and Indian ways for spiritual guidance. The Beatles, their wives and friends were among them.

Teresa was not keen to be filmed 'in action', but finally she agreed, 'if this TV programme is going to help people love better.' It took five days to make the 50-minute documentary. When Muggeridge returned to England, Mother Teresa wrote to him, 'I can't tell you how big a sacrifice it was to accept the making of a film – but I am glad now that I did so because it has brought us all closer to God. In your own way try to make the world conscious that it is never too late to do something beautiful for God.'

Those last four words became the title of the black-and-white film that was first shown in 1969. Millions of viewers were now astonished to see for themselves what the Missionaries of Charity were doing among Calcutta's poor. TV cameras even filmed inside Nirmal Hriday and, although it was very murky in there, the resulting pictures seemed to be bathed in a golden light. To some, this was nothing short of a miracle, making Mother Teresa herself almost saintly.

INTERNATIONAL RECOGNITION

By 1970 there were 585 Sisters in Mother Teresa's order, of whom 332 were fully-**professed** nuns. Year by year new recruits – from Venezuela, Malaysia, Nepal, Italy and many other countries – were swelling the ranks at an even greater rate than before. In addition, an increasing number of **lay** assistants belonged to the **order's** International Association of Co-Workers.

Among other projects, the Co-Workers encouraged the world's better-off children to help the starving poor of India. As a result of the 'bread campaign' in the UK, British boys and girls saved enough pennies to give 5000 Indian slum schoolchildren a daily slice of bread. Thousands of Danish children 'made beautiful sacrifices' to provide a daily glass of condensed milk.

Mother Teresa, as the head of such a successful international organization, won acclaim from people of all kinds. Among her supporters were prime ministers and other leading politicians whom she met on her travels. She was never overawed by 'important' people and if she felt that they could help with one of her projects she did not hesitate to let them know. She asked Indian Prime Minister Indira Gandhi if she could be a stewardess on Indian

Mother Teresa received an honorary degree in 1976, from her friend Indira Gandhi, the Indian Prime Minister.

Airlines – then she could keep in touch with all her **Missionary** homes without wasting money on air-fares. Mrs Gandhi responded in 1973 by giving her a free air pass.

A RELUCTANT HEROINE

Mother Teresa received a stream of awards and prizes in recognition of her work, ranging from the Pope John XXIII Peace Prize in 1971 to the American 'Master et Magister' Award in 1975. She was also given a number of titles from universities and colleges, including an honorary Doctorate of Divinity from Cambridge University in the UK. She took the **plaudits** with humility and good humour. 'I never know whether I should accept or not,' she once said, 'it means nothing to me. But it gives me a chance to speak of Christ to people who otherwise may not hear of him.' She knew, too, that when she spoke in public she usually managed to convert more listeners to join her worldwide **crusade** – and the poor could always use any prize money she won.

Mother Teresa at the 1979 ceremony where she received the Nobel Peace Prize.

NOBEL PRIZE WINNER

Throughout the 1970s Malcolm Muggeridge and others campaigned hard for Mother Teresa to be given the Nobel Peace Prize. In 1972, when the judges in Oslo, Norway, asked Muggeridge what she had done for world peace, he replied, 'by dedicating her life wholly to Christ, by seeing in every suffering soul her Saviour and treating them accordingly,... she was...along with her **Missionaries** of Charity, a sort of power-house of love in the world.'

But in that year, in 1975 and again in 1977, the **lucrative** and **prestigious** prize went to someone else. 'I had a good laugh,' Mother Teresa remarked after the third disappointment. 'It will come only when Jesus thinks it is time. We have all calculated to build two hundred homes for the lepers if it comes, so our people will have to do the praying.' Then at last, in 1979, she won.

'MOTHER OF THE WORLD'

In December 1979 Mother Teresa went to Oslo to receive her medal and a cheque for £90,000 – as well as a further £36,000 raised by young people in

Norway. Usually there would have been a celebration banquet – costing £3000 – but she asked the organizers to cancel it and spend the money on the poor instead. As a Nobel Prize winner, her fame soared to even greater heights. 'You have been the Mother of Bengal,' Jyoti Basu, an Indian politician, told her at a special reception, 'now you are the Mother of the World.'

Mother Teresa took every public opportunity to spread the word about her work.

The year 1979 has not been a year of peace. Disputes and conflicts between nations, peoples and **ideologies** have been conducted with all the accompanying extremes of inhumanity and cruelty. We have witnessed wars, the unrestrained use of violence,... fanaticism hand in hand with cynicism... contempt for human life and dignity... The Norwegian Nobel Committee has considered it right and appropriate, precisely in this year, in their choice of Mother Teresa to remind the world of the words spoken by Fridtjof Nansen: "Love of one's neighbour is realistic policy."'

From the address of Professor John Sannes, chairman of the Norwegian Nobel Committee, in Oslo 1979

TOO MANY CHILDREN?

Mother Teresa always spoke from the heart but, despite her obvious sincerity, her views sometimes surprised people and even seemed insensitive. On receiving her Nobel Prize in Oslo, she made headlines with a speech condemning abortion. She called it 'the greatest destroyer of peace today… because it is a direct war, a direct killing, direct murder by the mother herself.' Her Sisters, she said, had saved thousands of lives by telling Indian clinics, hospitals and police stations, 'Please don't destroy the child; we will take the child… And also we are doing another thing which is very beautiful. We are teaching our beggars, our leprosy patients, our slum dwellers, our people of the street, natural family planning.' This meant using the **rhythm method**, the only kind of contraception approved by the Roman Catholic Church.

'Human life must be respected and protected absolutely from the moment of conception… Since it must be treated from conception as a person, the **embryo** must be defended in its integrity, cared for, and healed as far as possible like any other human being.'
From 1992 Catholic Church Catechism

MURDER OR MERCY KILLING?

In a heavily overpopulated world, not everyone agreed with views like these. Mother Teresa was called unrealistic for holding them. Feminists claimed that it was a woman's right to decide whether

or not to have children. But she would not **compromise**. At a Prayer Breakfast with US President Clinton in 1995 she flatly stated, 'As I am the pencil of God, I know what God likes and does not like. He does not like abortion and contraception.' Someone present later said, 'Many in the audience clearly felt that this was arrogance to the point of rudeness, but there were also some, I know, who felt a deep appreciation of what she was saying.'

Some of the children from Shishu Bavan, the **Missionaries** of Charity's home for abandoned children.

'Mother Teresa told Malcolm Muggeridge that there could never be too many children in India because God always provides. 'He provides for the flowers and the birds and for everything in the world that he has created. And those little children are his life. There can never be enough.' Charming though that is, it somehow misses the point. Of course, once children exist everything must be done to look after them. But, sadly, there is not always the provision for them... Ten years after this comment Mother Teresa admitted to a Newsweek reporter that overpopulation was a serious problem.'

From *Mother Teresa – Beyond the Image* by Anne Sebba, 1997

GOD'S GLOBETROTTER

In the years after Mother Teresa won the Nobel Peace Prize, political and business leaders were keener than ever to speak with her and be photographed with her at 54a Lower Circular Road – and then pour more funds into the **Missionaries'** coffers. She also received many more invitations from abroad to make speeches or to visit refugee camps in the world's trouble-spots – where she did much more than simply talk.

BACK HOME

In 1980 she even had the chance to return to Skopje, the town where she was born. So much had

'What stunned everyone was her energy and efficiency. She saw the problem, fell to her knees and prayed for a few seconds and then she was rattling off a list of supplies she needed – nappies, plastic pants, chamber pots. The problem is that in wartime most of the attention is focused on the casualties. But the blind, the deaf, the insane and the spastics tend to be forgotten just when they need help the most. Mother Teresa understood that right away.'
An International Red Cross official in Beirut in the war-torn Lebanon, 1982

happened since her departure at the age of eighteen. Her brother Lazar had left the **Balkans** too. In 1960 Mother Teresa had arranged to meet him when she was in Italy, but she was never able to see her mother and sister Age again. For decades they had lived in Albania, which had become an **atheist** Communist country whose borders were closed to most of the rest of the world.

During the 1980s, Mother Teresa was sometimes away from India for ten months of each year, but her **order's** work showed no sign of falling off. In 1979 there were 158 Missionaries of Charity houses in the world. In the next year fourteen more were opened, then eighteen in the next. By 1982 there were also 81 homes for dying **destitutes** admitting 13,000 people, and six million sick people were being treated by 670 mobile clinics.

SAINT AMONG THE SINNERS?

In the mid–1980s Mother Teresa caused a stir in New York. She arranged for three violent prisoners to be transferred from Sing Sing Prison into the Sisters' care at a special hospital. This was because the prisoners had the fatal disease AIDS.

'We plan to give them tender loving care because each one is Jesus in a distressing disguise,' she said. 'We are not here to·sit in judgement on these people, to decide blame or guilt. Our mission is to help them to make their dying days more tolerable and we have Sisters who are dedicated to do that.' But according to the doctor at the hospital, the Sisters had no idea what AIDS was or how to deal with the disease. 'The crucifix on your chest isn't going to protect you,' the doctor warned them. 'God will provide,' Mother Teresa replied.

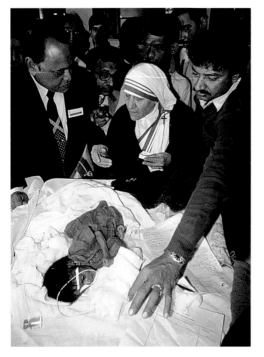

Mother Teresa and a sick child in Bhopal, India.

ETHIOPIAN MERCY MISSION

In 1985 Mother Teresa visited Ethiopia at the height of its terrible famine. Her order was already at work in the capital Addis Ababa, and running a feeding programme and hospital

Rock star Bob Geldof offered to perform a benefit concert in India for the order. Mother Teresa said there was no need – God would provide.

in the province of Wollo; now she wanted to see what more she could do. The **media** were fascinated by her meeting with rock star Bob Geldof, who had raised huge amounts of money for Ethiopia with his **Band Aid** project. 'What you do I could not do,' she told him, 'and what I do you could not do. But as long as it is clear in your heart and your mind, then it is God's will to see us through.'

'She was astonishingly tiny. When I went to greet her I found that I towered more than two feet above her. She was a battered, wizened woman. The thing that struck me most forcefully was her feet. Her **habit** was clean and well cared for but her sandals were beaten-up pieces of leather from which her feet protruded, gnarled and misshapen as old tree roots... [then when he bent to kiss her] she bowed her head so swiftly that I was obliged to kiss the top of her **wimple**. It disturbed me. I found out later that she only let lepers kiss her.'

From *Is That It?*, the **autobiography** of Bob Geldof, 1986

A Political Animal?

In his 1994 book *An Intimate History of Humanity*, Theodore Zeldin of Oxford University wrote that, in the modern world, 'Power no longer ensures respect. Even the most powerful person in the world, the President of the United States, is not powerful enough to command everybody's respect; he probably has less than Mother Teresa, whom nobody is obliged to obey.' Many politicians must have envied Mother Teresa for the global respect she enjoyed. But she herself was careful to treat politicians well. This was partly because she knew they had the power and **resources** to help her in her work. By being respectful, she could also hope to influence their other actions.

'Dear President George Bush and President Saddam Hussein, I come to you with tears in my eyes and God's love in my heart to plead to you for the poor and those who will become poor if the war that we all dread and fear happens. I beg you with my whole heart to work for, to labour for God's peace and to be reconciled with one another… In the short term there may be winners and losers in this war that we all dread, but that never can, nor ever will justify the suffering, pain and loss of life which your weapons will cause.'

From a letter to the US and Iraqi presidents on the eve of the Gulf War, 1991

ABOVE POLITICS?

Sometimes Mother Teresa's willingness to greet and be greeted by political leaders caused concern. In 1980 she visited Haiti, one of the world's poorest countries, yet she had nothing but praise for rich and **despotic** President Duvalier and his First Lady. Then in 1989 she was finally allowed to enter Albania, where she laid a bouquet on the tombstone of Enver Hoxha, the country's brutal Communist ruler who had died four years before. According to Dr Jack Preger, who once worked for her in Calcutta, 'Mother Teresa is prepared to shake hands with any type of murderer who happens to be in political power.' But she usually had her reasons. After 'hobnobbing' with the Albanian **authorities**, for example, she was allowed to set up two houses where her Sisters could start work in that desperately needy country.

PROBLEMS IN THE NINETIES

As Mother Teresa entered her ninth decade, her own health became an important issue. Since founding her **order**, she had pushed herself extraordinarily hard. Although prone to sickness as a child and younger woman, it was almost as if she did not *allow* herself to become ill during the second, highly active part of her life. But in September 1989 she suffered a serious heart attack and had to undergo major surgery. Two years later she was treated for heart disease and bacterial pneumonia. Despite her frailty, she kept on travelling and, in 1993, when in Rome, she fell and broke her ribs. Within months she fell critically ill again with malaria, complicated by heart and lung problems.

In her later years Mother Teresa's health was clearly deteriorating.

WHO COULD TAKE HER PLACE?

As early as 1990, she told the Pope that she thought she should resign. But as the figurehead for the **Missionaries** of Charity, many people believed her to be irreplaceable. She was so well-known that she gave the order a wonderfully clear identity – and her matchless reputation encouraged people all over the world to contribute funds.

Mother Teresa herself had never groomed anyone to take her place. 'Wait until I die and then see,' she would say. Some said that she had always found it hard to **delegate** responsibility. She alone decided, for example, whether a door thousands of miles away should be painted blue or white.

Ill though she was, she continued to lead her order until 1997. Then on 13 March, after weeks of discussions, the Missionaries of Charity announced that a solution had been found. Mother Teresa would stay on as head in name, but another nun would take on the day-to-day chores of running the order. The new 'Superior General' was to be Sister Nirmala, a shy 63-year-old woman who had converted from Hinduism to Christianity.

As events turned out, this arrangement was to last for less than a year, for on 5 September 1997 – the day of Princess Diana's funeral – Mother Teresa died of a heart attack at the Mother House.

Sister Nimala, who had the hard task of succeeding Mother Teresa as head of the Missionaries of Charity.

Going Home to God

At the time of Mother Teresa's death, her order had more than 4000 Sisters and nearly 600 homes in around 130 different countries. But the great sense of loss was felt by many millions more around the world. Her **embalmed** body was placed under a glass dome in St Thomas' church, Calcutta, and in the next week huge crowds filed past to pay their last respects. Meanwhile it was announced that Mother Teresa would be given the honour of a state funeral, which would be arranged by the army. To some this seemed a peculiar outcome for a woman who had worked so tirelessly all her life for peace.

On Saturday 13 September her body was transported to the 12,000-seater Netaji indoor stadium, where 400 international dignitaries were among the mourners. The four-mile route was lined by 100,000 people. Then millions watched the two and half a hour funeral service on TV. Representatives of the six major faiths in India – Christian, Hindu, Muslim, Sikh, Buddhist and Parsee – spoke in praise of Mother Teresa. Finally, with rain teeming down, her coffin was taken for private burial in the Mother House. A 21-gun salute announced that the body had been lowered into the ground then four soldiers sounded bugles. On her grave was carved, 'Love one another as I have loved you.'

The coffin of Mother Teresa at her funeral in September 1997.

WAS SHE A SAINT?

Before she died, Mother Teresa spoke without fear of 'going home to God'. She fully expected St Peter to recognize her as she approached heaven's gates 'and he will say "but what have you done, Mother Teresa, filling up paradise with all your poor people?"' She herself was believed by many to be a saint during her lifetime, yet saints have to be officially declared by the highest officials of the Roman Catholic Church, and the making of a saint is a very long, slow process. Usually it does not even begin until the person has been dead for five years, but Cardinal Joseph Ratzinger – a close adviser to Pope John Paul II – has hinted that in Mother Teresa's case this process could be 'less long'. Few will be surprised if the 'Saint of the Slums' is made an official saint very soon.

'DON'T LOOK FOR NUMBERS'

Few people publicly criticized Mother Teresa or her work until the last few years of her life. For decades she was seen – especially in Europe and the USA – as an almost holy figure herself. It hardly seemed right to find fault, since she was so clearly a selfless, decent woman who was doing a great deal of good.

But as the writer Anne Sebba pointed out towards the end of Mother Teresa's life, 'after fifty years, the world of charity has moved on. Those who give are, by and large, no longer prepared to do so in the vague hope that it does some good somewhere.' Some critics now believed that instead of helping individual people who were poor or sick, the **Missionaries** of Charity should have tried to attack poverty and disease at its root: treat the cause, not the symptom.

Mother Teresa did not share this view. When she heard her efforts described as small drops in the ocean of need, she would reply, 'I do not add up. I only subtract from the total number of poor or dying. With children one dollar saves a life. Could you say one dollar buys a life? No, but it is used to save it.' According to her authorized biographer, Kathryn Spink, 'The call to change social structures and deal with the root cause of collective problems was a valid one but it was for others."Begin in a small way,"– she directed those who worked with her."Don't look for numbers."'

The Gospel of Love

Pope John Paul II, a close friend and supporter of Mother Teresa, was too ill to attend her funeral, so he sent the Vatican Secretary of State, Cardinal Angelo Sodano, in his place. In his tribute, Sodano said that Mother Teresa had been fully aware of criticisms of her. 'It has been said that Mother Teresa might have done more to fight the causes of poverty in the world. She would shrug as if saying, 'while you go on discussing causes and explanations, I will kneel beside the poorest of the poor and attend to their needs. The dying, the handicapped and defenceless unborn… need a loving presence and a caring hand'. Mother Teresa of Calcutta understood fully the Gospel of love.

A young boy, with a photo of Mother Teresa, watches her funeral procession in September 1997.

MOTHER TERESA – TIMELINE

1910	Agnes Gonxha Bojaxhiu born in Skopje
1928	(September) Agnes leaves to join the Sisters of Loreto in Ireland
	(December) Sister Mary Teresa (Agnes) sails for India
1929	Sister Teresa starts teaching in Darjeeling
1931	Sister Teresa takes her first **vows** of poverty, **chastity**, obedience, and is sent to Calcutta to teach
1937	Sister Teresa takes her final vows and become Principal of St Mary's school
1946	Sister Teresa hears the 'call within a call' and asks to leave the convent to help the poor by living among them
1948	Sister Teresa, wearing a white **sari**, leaves the convent to begin her new work
1950	Pope approves the founding of Mother Teresa's **Missionaries** of Charity **Order**
1952	Nirmal Hriday, Home for the Dying, set up
1953	Missionaries move into their Mother House in Calcutta
1955	Shishu Bavan, the first children's home, opens
1960	Mother Teresa begins a period of extensive foreign travel
1965	Missionaries' first overseas house opens, in Venezuela
1969	*Something Beautiful for God* TV **documentary** shown
1975	United Nations Ceres medal struck in Mother Teresa's honour
1979	Mother Teresa wins the Nobel Peace Prize

1990 Sick Mother Teresa suggests to the Pope that she should resign, but does not

1997 (March) Mother Teresa finally gives up the day-to-day running of the order

(September) Mother Teresa dies – and the campaign begins to make her a saint

Kindly thank the people of the whole world and the woodland people for all their prayer and tender love and care I have received God bless you M Teresa mc

A message of thanks from Mother Teresa. She wrote it in 1989, during her convalescence after heart problems while staying at the Woodland Nursing Home in Calcutta.

GLOSSARY

affluent rich

aristocratic noble, high-born

atheist not believing in God or gods

authorities people who hold power

autobiography a book written by a person about their own life

Balkans south-eastern region of Europe

Band Aid money-raising project featuring pop musicians, led by Bob Geldof

Benediction a special Roman Catholic service

biography a book about a person's life

bustees Indian slum districts

charitable generous

chastity agreement not to have sexual relations, marry or have children

communion the taking of bread and wine in a church service

compound area of land in which a building stands

compromise become less forceful in holding a view

crusade a vigorous campaign to achieve something worthwhile

delegate to hand responsibility to someone else in an organization

despotic harsh in ruling

destitutes extremely poor people

devout deeply religious

documentary (TV) a programme about a real-life person or thing

donations gifts (usually of money)

embalmed preserved from decay

embryo the earliest formation of a baby inside its mother

equerry officer in a royal household

Eurasian person with one European and one Asian parent

grant a legal handing-over of something, often money

habit the dress worn by members of a religious order

hospitality kindness to guests or strangers

humanitarian person who tries to improve human welfare

idealism aiming high in your thinking and planning

ideology set of ideas about how people should lead their lives

independent (country) ruling over itself, not part of another country

Jesuit a member of an order of the Roman Catholic Church founded in 1534

lay (brother or sister) not a full member of a religious order

lucrative money-making

mass Catholic church service

media plural of medium (of communication), e.g. newspapers, TV, radio

missionary religious person who goes to help and teach the poor abroad

novice (nun) a trainee sister

order (religious) group of men or women who bind themselves with vows to devote themselves to religious aims

pastor minister in charge of church or congregation

patronage support (sometimes financial) given by a supporter

pilgrimage journey to a sacred place as an act of religious devotion

plaudits praises, applause

prestigious well worth having, of very high reputaion, valuable

professed (nuns) nuns who have taken the vows of their religious order

Protestant Reformation revolutionary event in sixteenth-century Europe which led to the setting up of first 'Protestant' Churches alongside Catholic ones

redemption being saved or 'bought back'

resources (financial) funds

rhythm method system of contraception based on avoiding sexual intercourse at times of the month when the woman is ovulating (producing eggs)

rule code of discipline observed by a religious order

rupees money units of India and Pakistan

sari traditional dress of Hindu women, consisting of single piece of cloth

smallpox contagious virus disease

sodality a Roman Catholic religious society

untouchables Hindus who are born into a group low down the social ladder

vows solemn and serious promises

wimple nun's head-dress

INDEX